Pressures

of

Potential

Julia Dane

BookLeaf
Publishing

Presentation by *BookLeaf Publishing*

Web: www.bookleafpub.com

E-mail: info@bookleafpub.com

ISBN: 9789395621137

First edition 2022

DEDICATION

To those who understand,

and to those who don't.

PREFACE

Having been told to live up to potential, years were spent working towards figuring out what that was or what it looked like. There is still so far to go. Burnout in medicine is real. Even students struggle with learning to incorporate a diamond's worth of pressure in their day. This collection hopes to bring to light some small moments that turn into a larger burden from the viewpoint and limited understanding of a student just starting this path (while having already put 24 years in). Some parts will be light, but hopefully, you can feel the pressures too.

To-Do List

Pencils down
well,
now it's a laptop I click shut.
This marks the completion of exams.
Gone are the days of marching up front
turning in the results of my knowledge
proud of the work I've done
at least now it's over,
I sit at home
all alone
proud of the work I've done
painfully busy for terribly long.
Nothing new to study.
Nothing now to complete.
What to do with all this new
beautiful,
stressless,
glistening time?
dishes

Just a Dream

Racing around the school
hunting for a room
an exam for which I have not yet prepped
this will be my doom
how could I forget such a vital date?
I'll never learn all the material at this rate
Why as I'm running,
 I don't know where I'm going
sweat from the stress
through my shirt is showing
Can't even think
of what this test is about
I try to ask a friend
 but am inept to shout
Pressures and stresses grasp my chest
I thought it was summer why can't I rest?!
Oh wait,
I wake

Seconds of Summer

12 weeks of summer!
It's nice to see friends again
a chance to binge all the shows on my list,
but will I have a chance?
Still need to pad my resume-
should I also fit in
an internship, shadowing, and research?
8 weeks of summer
need to relax
it's summer, why can't I relax?
No,
you are not the first person to tell me...
I'm uptight.
yes,
it's my break; I'm enjoying it.
Am I enjoying a break?
4 weeks of summer
time to start preparing for the Fall semester.
Am I ready?
Didn't summer just begin?
Still so much more to do before my mind
belongs to the school
2 weeks...
one.

Classes start tomorrow.
Who would guess, but there will be a quiz
take me back to May-
I forgot to use my summer.

Learning from Another

5

Boundless trust is placed
in the students that came before
materials and links and tips passed down
bridged between generations
is a jaunted understanding
of personal exertion.
To take time
from their own overwhelmed schooling
looking up to them and what they aspire,
how to learn massive amounts
in just mere minutes
beholden for each dribble of instruction
habitually more helpful than even instructors.

Teaching One Another

After hours and hours and hours,
I should know this by now
same tests taken; same lectures heard
my turn to pass down
what I have earned to know
wish I could remember.
Extra hours and hours and hours,
learning it again once more
success means they learn it too.
Knowing each and every in and out
to answer questions
you didn't know could come,
and hope you aren't completely wrong.

Take a Break

long have I studied
peaceful rest eludes my mind
please stop reviewing

For Later

Showering
Shaving
Laundry
Appointments
Groceries
Brunch
Cooking
Dusting
Scrubbing
Sweeping
Running
Exercising
Resting
These things will not be done today,
next exam is a week away.

6 Foot Physician

Can one learn to be a true physician
not learning the face of each and every patient
these masks bring about such disconnect,
when the basis of our interaction
is to try and connect.
What additional clues might be missed
when my exam is obstructed?
My patient no less than 6 feet away
as my encounter is conducted.
They worry and fear for a disease I know
naught
Corona is rare, or so I was taught.
Once they came in for just a sore throat,
but now clinics and ERs
are this virus's scapegoat
our patients are ignoring emergencies every day
while their physician is standing
 just six feet away

One Day One Lesson

The skills acquired
reach to assist later on
for now, I practice

No Time for Me; No Time for You

Once upon a time,
you were my everything.
Days nights weeks and years
time consumed serendipitously,
distractions lacked to tear away
the tunnel vision
laughter, excitement, glee
all we ever understood.
Weekends were for exploration of our world and of
one another
there was never a noticeable
nor immediate change
weekends are now for drifting distantly away
from one another.
In the same home, we don't live together
shared are our beds, our food, our air
but not our thoughts, concerns, frustrations
or even our time.
What's mine is yours
so, what I do not have, neither do you.
We wait,
maybe more time will give us more time
how long to wait?
It has been days and weeks and nights and years.
There is still no time for me.
Hoping,
once upon a time is upon a time again.

C Won't be Enough for Me

"C's get degrees"
That is not a grading acceptable for me.
If anything short of perfection persists
my hopes and dreams will slowly desist.
This path ahead is tiring and fraught
why this is the journey
I reached outand sought,
piling pillars of knowledge deep in my brain
to hope the answers will drizzle down
easily as rain.
Constant calculations to ensure my grade
so once finals are listed
I hope to not be dismayed,
Even while walking and dancing
through each situation
my mind has reached saturation.
For this student, failure is not an option
a C is nothing short of a toxin.

Inside Out

Let me help you feel better;

I feel like I've been run over

I can show you how to do this;

I had to figure it out myself

You should try to get more rest;

I have not slept in three days

Fresh air might lift your mood;

I don't even know what season it is

Let's try to cut back a few drinks a week;

I pour a glass at the end of my day

A healthy diet can improve overall health;

The pizza place has my order saved

Do not take a medication that is not prescribed;

Thankfully my buddy put in an order

Let's not get worried before tests arrive;

No news at this point would be better

It's great that we made a plan together;

Wikipedia must be a better diagnostic tool than I

I am sorry you have had that experience;

I've seen it 10 times, am I jaded?

Post Exam

Now past abundant hours locked solitarily away
broken down literates are excited to play.
While for weeks, we have remained soft and mild
this freedom allows a chance to go wild!
Get it out while you can, for we only get a day.

Firehose

A popular opinion:
medical school is like drinking water
straight from a hose,
not a garden hose
a firehose
150 square inches of pounds of pressure
of water
at once.
A pool with that water
could be filled
in just 10 minutes
swimming through an overflow of material
a chance to drown
in just the water
from a single hose?
That.
is a lie...
It is not a mere single hose
spritzing a spray. 
Using personal,
extensive,
bouts of research
and contemplation
the true comparison through calculation
is not one
but rather,
a metric ton.

A Choice Was Made

When you grow up...
an answer that every child must have ready
in their back pocket.
Every adult will ask,
they will expect greatness
and blandness
in a defining response.
Vet, doctor, astronaut, firefighter
so grand and unoriginal,
but what else does a child know to aspire for?
We all wish to be grand and original.
It matters none that the answer may change.
All expect so much to show promise
to show potential,
that bar is set so high,
so quickly, so young.
So much to live up to
terrified of falling short
you've given your answer already,
no taking it back now.
It turns you into where you go
a path planned out.
As you learn what you like,
and what you can handle,
maybe the two are not the same.

Midst of a Question

17

Trendles roped in the depths of neurons
stretching to be pulled out
analysis and reason bow before panic
breathe brain,
think.

Nothing Could Go Wrong

Here I am.
Delicately stomping on fragile steps
to finally reach the stairwell's peak
somehow, a lightyear away from a finish line,
at least I made it this far.
Reaching to grasp the bar raised incredibly high
trotting along my way.
Still considerable time for heaps to go wrong:
as a woman of childbearing age
children are precious.
My time is precious, and I am still selfish.
Reading along my list of fears,
financial struggles persist every day
planning a dish alongside ramen
rent, at least, is paid.
Scrap coins piled together
piecemealing nights out
must keep up appearances
No-
that is not where money belongs,
but it's a welcome reprieve.
really the greatest thing
that may go awry

they find out I do not actually belong.
Truly not as brilliant
as I have led them to believe.
Fooled by a resume
of accomplishments and valor
fooled by work ethic and stamina
maybe they may find me out.
Until then,
for now
here I am.

Who They Want

Expectations are higher
than the crown placed
can be held up.
Precariously perched on
the pedestal provided,
everyone is watching.

The World Around Goes On

At the point of cap and gown
we are sitting unsteadily on the same page.
Peak age of 18,
the world gently waiting
on the tip of our tongue.
While peers explored careers
in a hometown
settling down starting families
beginning a beautiful raw life,
I shushed the world and asked it to wait.
Hesitant to leave classroom doors
knowledge is power
intent to wield it all.
What kind of knowledge is power
if I don't know not how to change a tire?
Kindergarten friends see their brood off to
the first day of school,
I am on my 19th first day of school
the world gave me a push
I sat and pulled back.
Wait, I beg

it is not time for me yet
sighing, it moved right on along.
Undergraduate peers;
married and contented
learning from books
does not teach emotions
centuries to go
in my comfortable classroom.
Youth is fleeting.
With great power,
comes great responsibility
and sacrifice.
I asked the world to wait for far too long
it went on,
too late to ask now.

Softly Speak Louder

The strangest thing happened.
I was telling a story
that wasn't quite interesting
and there arose a prickling,
profound
feeling.
A tingling sensation tickling my shoulder.
The sensation of eyes staring closely at me.
I was telling a story,
but were they actually listening?
I noticed then as the room was silent
my words the only ones to hear.
I became focused on the words
embarrassed that they were not
abundantly special,
Or fascinating,
but no matter the words
receivers were quiet and attentive,
listening to me.
That was the strangest thing.
Used to being spoken over,

overlooked,

unnoticed

perhaps my status has finally changed.

Not simply a female in a room,

but now

a powerful voice with something to say.

Even if this particular story

held no true value

maybe something else slips out that will.

It's strange to be heard.

Now words,

spoken just as softly as before,

impart with a significantly greater volume.

472 Miles

Taking on a task
I know I'm not alone,
I've built up an army
they have made this place my home.

www.ingramcontent.com/pod-product-compliance
Lightning Source LLC
Chambersburg PA
CBHW070731160726
48003CB00006BA/2440